Don't Feed Elephants

How to Achieve Personal and Professional Success

Carol Farabee
Colette Williams Draper

Farabee Publishing
P O Box 322, Chandler, Arizona, 85244
www.Farabeepublishing.com

Printed in the United States of America

Book Cover designed by David Mor

ISBN: 978-1-64826-342-2

Table of Contents

Chapter 1 Introduction

Walt Disney was told he lacked creativity.

WD-40 got its name because the 40th try was the one that worked.

Bubble wrap was originally intended to be wallpaper, and then housing insulation. It wasn't until IBM used it for packaging its new computers that the ubiquitous material became widely known and used.

Before the doctor came in to deliver results of the latest round of bloodwork tests, Nadine knew what she was going to hear. She had heard it before.

The fatigue, shortness of breath, pain in her joints wasn't the result of old age – she was only 45. It was because she was severely overweight.

She needed to make a change and make it soon. If not, she would not live to see her children grow up or travel to all the exotic locations she had dreamed of for years.

Nadine signed up for a "lose the weight and we'll give your money back" fitness programs. She wasn't sure it would work, but what the hell, she'd give it a try. It was grueling and painful.

She missed eating her favorite foods and drinking soda. She missed her muscles not screaming in agony with every squat. After a year of setbacks and charge forwards, Nadine lost over 150 pounds and felt better than she ever had in her life.

Success is a frame of mind. It is small, personal triumphs known only to the individual. It's a grand display with much public praise.

Success is not about how much money you have in the bank, the title on your business card, or the degree hanging on your wall. Success is about the feeling you get when you have achieved a goal.

How do we know if our vision is right? We don't... but if you follow the right path for the right reasons you are going to find your way.

Regardless of what success means to you, how you attain that worthy goal is universal. This book explores the various avenues to reaching success and how to work your way around the roadblocks you will certainly encounter.

"Success is not final; failure is not fatal: it is the courage to continue that counts."
~ Winston Churchill

"You just can't beat the person who won't give up."
~ Babe Ruth

"Successful men and women keep moving. They make mistakes, but they don't quit."
~ Conrad Hilton

Chapter 2 – Your Definition of Success Matters

How you define success is going to be different than the person sitting next to you. It will be different from your parents, siblings, friends, and co-workers. Take a deep breath and repeat until you believe it: Only you can define what your success means.

*If you carefully consider what you want to be
said of you in the funeral experience,
you will find your definition of success.*
~ Stephen Covey

Section 1: Know Where You Want to Go

What is your goal? Is it writing a book, learning a new skill, winning a Nobel prize? Before you can figure *how* to succeed, you must know what it is you want to achieve.

Section 2: What Matters the Most to You?

Individuals have different motivators that impact the goals you set for yourself. For some people, it's helping others through volunteerism. For others, it is fame, fortune, and having their name in lights. And yet for others, it's a quiet comfortable life. Whatever your motivator – it's important.

Define success on your own terms, achieve it by your own rules, and build a life you're proud to live."
~ Anne Sweeney.

"Success is the result of perfection, hard work, learning from failure, loyalty, and persistence."
~ Colin Powell

Chapter 3 – Failure IS an Option

Two of the greatest baseball hitters of all time, Ty Cobb and Ted Williams, finished their esteemed careers with batting averages at .366 and .344 respectively. This means that they were struck out, popped out, or thrown out 65 times out of 100 – a 65% failure rate!

Success is a lousy teacher. It seduces smart people into thinking they can't lose.
~ Bill Gates

Section 1: Redefining the Meaning of Failure

The traditional meaning of failure is "lack of success; failing, being an unsuccessful person or thing." Let's shift our perception and perspective by redefining failure to mean: "the starting line, part of process, or on the path to success".

The common element is failing is not the product but the people working on the project or product.

They lose their confidence, determination and follow through to make it happen.

Section 2: Stagnation

Not trying, does not mean you have failed. It means you didn't try. Period. Stagnation is neither failing or succeeding – it's standing still and hoping for the best. Stagnation sucks.

Section 3: Overcoming Failure: Reflect, Accept, and Move On

It is okay to feel sadness and anger if you are not achieving what you hoped you would. What's not okay is turning that anger towards yourself for failing. Many give up after the first sign of disappointment because they did not hit their deadline or goal. Re-examine where you are in the process, evaluate what did not work and why, and then regroup to move on.

"Failure is success in progress,"
~ Albert Einstein

"It does not matter how slowly you go as long as you do not stop."
~ Confucius

Chapter 4 – Conscious, Subconscious, Unconscious Ambitions

We are complex in our thinking as we have three levels of consciousness that define the decisions we make. We have feelings, thoughts, and perceptions that come from past experiences buried deep in our levels of consciousness. We do not identify with these because we accept them as part of who we are. We live by them as well as live with them.

*To be yourself in a world that is constantly
trying to make you something else
is the greatest accomplishment.*
~ Ralph Waldo Emerson

Section 1: Conscious Mind

Your conscious mind is what most people associate with who you are. When you look in the mirror the person looking back is a very superficial view.

This is the top level of who you are that everyone else sees, but it is only the tip of who you really are.

Section 2: Subconscious Mind

Your subconscious is 95% of who you are and is very powerful. If we realize and think about who we really are we can make changes in attitude and life choices.

Section3: Unconscious Mind

This is a very important piece of who we are that is a secret from most people. It is not talked about very much. This is the foundation of who we are – the memories, habits, and beliefs since birth. This is the truth of who we really are.

"All the things that happen in our lives are tied to the unconscious. This is because it is, more than anything, the matrix of our repetitions."
~ Gabriel Rolón

This above all: to thine own self be true, And it must follow, as the night the day, Thou canst not then be false to any man. Farewell, my blessing season this in thee!
~ Polonius last words to his son in Shakespeare's play of Hamlet.

Chapter 5 – Success is a Marathon… With Some Hurdles

Anthony was born addicted to the drugs his mother took while pregnant. Lack of oxygen during birth resulted in a delayed development disorder.

He struggled daily with tasks that other young children seemed to accomplish with ease. At five years old, he learned to walk.

At seven, he read his first words. In his short life, Anthony has fallen more than he has walked. Those falls never hurt as much as the thought of never being able to run had.

Our greatest weakness lies in giving up.
The most certain way to succeed is always to try
just one more time.
~ Thomas A. Edison

Section 1: Identifying Success Blockers

Ask yourself what's really stopping you from succeeding. Is it money, education, time, patience, lack of support?

Identify what's holding back your success and make a plan to overcome them.

Section 2: Excuses vs. Reasons

An excuse is the little voice in the back of our head (and sometimes spoked out loud) that nay-says our ideas for success. An excuse holds you back from trying. A reason is the result of a cause and effect reaction. Figure out the difference and stop listening to the little voices telling you not to try.

Section 3: Fear, Uncertainty, and Doubt

Sometimes we think that success comes from doing things a certain way. That you can only achieve success if you follow the established pattern that others have followed before you. Trying something new is scary and unsure.

Forging your own path to success is much like working your way through the woods on your own for the first time. Imagine if Lewis and Clark had said: "that river looks too rough, let's stop here."

Chapter 6 – Your Biggest Critic is… YOU

You have high expectations of yourself and want to succeed. That's as it should be. Having a goal and wanting to reach it is what moves us forward.

Remember, however, that we are all running on what we believe success is and can be. What we need to understand is that we are all different.

We all have our special gifts and we are not all the same. Being hard on yourself leads to negative thoughts and feelings of self-criticism, self-judgment, self-blame, and other feelings and thoughts hinder your growth.

Your harshest critic is always going to be yourself.
Don't ignore that critic but don't give it more attention than it deserves.
~ Michael Ian Black

Section 1: Expectation vs. Reality

You are on the starting line of a 5K run. This is the longest run you have never entered. What are your expectations? What is your measurement of success?

Since this is the first time you've ever run a race like this, winning may not be a realistic goal.

Finishing is good enough. Finishing without puking at kilometer 3? Even better!

Section 2: Asking for Help Is Not A Sign of Weakness

We listen, learn and act on what we know is true not from guessing but from asking the right questions.

We are not always going to get the answer we are looking for and we do not have to accept the answer we are given.

How will we know which answers to accept if we don't ask the questions?

Section 3: Acknowledge Your Accomplishments

Everyone has accomplished something. Make a list and check it twice. Give yourself a chance to say, "Good Job."

Do not be afraid to congratulate yourself on a job well done. It is not about ego – it's about acknowledging your success and finding encouragement for finding more.

Chapter 7 A Failure to Plan is a Plan to Fail

Make a goal. Write it down and study it. What do you need to do to make the goal happen?   All goals have identifiable milestones.

Each step you take on your path success is supported by the steps you previously took.

Breakdown all the steps, make them as easily attainable as possible. Each time you take the next step, you will know you are that much closer to your goal.

If you want to change the world, start off by making your bed. If you make your bed every morning, you will have accomplished the first task of the day.
It will give you a small sense of pride, and it will encourage you to do another task, and another, and another. And by the end of the day that one task completed will have turned into many tasks completed.
~ Retired Admiral and Former Navy Seal
William H. McRaven

*Section 1: Project Manage the **** Out of This!*

Be the project manager of your own success. You know what you want to achieve. Make a plan of how to do it… and follow through on that plan.

Section 2: That Was an Awesome Mistake

In 1856, chemist William Perkin was trying to make a synthetic version of quinine, a drug used to treat malaria. During his many failed experiments, he noticed that the gloopy mistake turned silk a beautiful shade of purple. And thus, synthetic fabric dye was invented.

Always remember sometimes our greatest failures are our greatest successes!

"Only those who dare to fail greatly can ever achieve greatly."
~ Robert F. Kennedy

Chapter 8 Readings

Carnegie, D. (1998). *How to Win Friends and Influence People.* Pocket Books.

Collins, J. (2004). *Built to Last: Successful Habits of Visionary Companies* Harper Business

Covey, S. (2013) *The 7 Habits of Highly Effective People: Powerful Lessons in Personal Change.* Simon & Schuster

Gladwell, M. (2002) *The Tipping Point: How Little Things Can Make a Big Difference.* Back Bay Books

Gladwell, M. (2007) *Blink.* Back Bay Books

Gladwell, M. (2011). *Outliers: The Story of Success.* Back Bay Book

Gladwell, M. (2015). *David and Goliath: Underdogs, Misfits, and the Art of Battling Giants.* Black Bay Books

Logan, D. (2011) *Tribal Leadership: Leveraging Natural Groups to Build a Thriving Organization.* Harper Review

Mandela, N. (2013). *Long Walk to Freedom.* Back Bay Books

Peale, N. V. (1952). *The Power of Positive Thinking.* Prentice-Hall